DEDICATION

Giving thanks to my Father in Heaven and my Lord and Savior, JESUS CHRIST, and the Power of the Holy Spirit, for their continued control of my life. To my Loving Wife Vivian for her support, and to a host of close Relatives and Friends who over the years, were my signpost, to keep me on God's straight and narrow road.

This book is dedicated to my children, my children's children and for generations to come.

Let those that favor my righteous cause and have pleasure in my uprightness shout for joy and be glad and say continually, Let the lord be magnified, who takes pleasure in the prosperity in his servant.

And my tongue shall talk of your righteousness, rightness and justice, and of [my reasons for] your praise all the day long.

Psalm 35: 27-28

A Note to the Pastor's and Spiritual Leaders

Home Churches International is here to assist you in the growth of your ministries, a kind of spiritual halfway house. There are millions of unchurched people and their families that know there is only one true and living God, our Lord and Savior Jesus Christ. But because of sin and other weaknesses of the flesh, they may be too ashamed to find or even attend a bible base traditional church. Sometimes the unchurched was never taught or never understood God's mercy and grace and unconditional love. Then there are the others that may have been faithful to the body. For some reason real or imagined in their own minds they were disgraced, disillusioned, or even discouraged by someone or something and left the church. So with this book and our internet ministries, empowered by God's Holy Spirit have the ability on their own time and reaching into their homes and into their hearts. We teach them how to self feed on the Word of God. To grow in wisdom and knowledge, to apply rightly His Word of Truth to their daily lives.

Then we will no longer be infants, tossed back and forth by the waves, and blown here and there by every wind of teaching and by the cunning and craftiness of men in their deceitful scheming. Instead, speaking the truth in love, we will in all things grow up into him who is the Head, that is, Christ. From him the whole body, joined and held together by every supporting ligament, grows and builds itself up in love, as each part does its work. (Ephesians 4:14-16 **NIV**)

As these new saints of God, with a renewed mind and now having a Holy Ghost gift of Discernment. These Re-Born Again committed Christians, will be tremendously valuable families to any ministry that would love them in and make them feel at home. If you currently have members in your congregation that you know are on the outside looking in. Then this book could be the tool the Lord could use to bring them in the Body of Christ.

Contact us: (For Ministries Multiple Purchases Discounts)

E-mail: hci1million@gmail.com
Blog: homechurchesonline.org

Check Here For Broadcast Times and Schedule
Website: homechurchesinternational.org

FOREWORD

I believe that God gave Pastor Bland a vision that is well needed, in our High-Technology world that we are now living in. With our computers, I-phones, I-pods, and I-pads, we can now connect to and get our e-mails, and watch TV. We can see movies, get the up to date weather report or news. Connect to our blogs, Twitter, Facebook and so much more.

I am not saying that all these are bad or evil, but I know for sure that much of it has been abused. Well, Pastor Bland is taking this High-Technology culture and using it for God's Glory. By bringing the Power of God and the teaching of His Word right into your homes.

I believe that in this book you have in your hands right now, as you read this forward, will open your eyes to much that is going on in our world, in our churches, and most important in our hearts.

We must know that our Lord is soon at hand. His coming is imminent. We need to use every means possible, to tell the world about God's Saving Grace, and to teach them about His Word. The vision God gave Pastor Bland, I believe, will do just that.

I would encourage you to read this book and see what God would want you to do, to help Pastor Bland fulfill the vision God gave him.

Pastor Jim D'Alessandro,
Senior Pastor of Calvary Chapel Jurupa Valley

Table of Contents

Introduction — 1

1. Attack on God's Institution — 3
2. The Gospel Sent to a Gentiles Home — 7
3. Your Household Saved by Inviting in the Word of God — 10
4. Sharing a Meal will give Joy and Favor with Men — 19
5. The Biblical Priorities And Occupying Until He Comes — 22
6. The Apostle Paul's Stand, Against False Teaching and Starts a Home Church — 33
7. Building a House that will Please The Lord? — 52
8. How Do We Get Started? — 57

    Prayer For Salvation and Peace — 61

The Return of

GOD'S POWER

"In Your Home"

INTRODUCTION

H– OLY perfect in a moral sense: pure in heart: religious: set apart for sacred use.

O– RACLES a medium or agency of divine revelation: a person of great wisdom: a response by God.

M– INISTERS a servant: one who serves at the altar: a Clergyman.

E– VANGELIST good news: gospel: to make acquainted with the gospel: to preach the gospel from place to place: a doctrine or principle (in morals or politics) regarded as certain to produce good results.

For a man to be HOLY, one needs to Pray and Repent daily, while watching what his eyes see and what his hands do and controlling what his tongue says, a man who does these things will be used mightily of God.

When a man studies God's Word it gives him Wisdom, Grace and Hope. The knowledge of the Word gives this man the supernatural ability to speak with power and great conviction to Exhort or Rebuke however the Holy Spirit moves him, this is being an Oracle of God.

A person who attends to the affairs of others as a servant. He works to build a bridge from man's corrupt soul to Salvation. He teaches others what he has in being an heir to all of what the Kingdom of God has to offer. This man is a MINISTER of God.

An EVANGELIST is a person with great boldness. His desire to preach the good news of the bible. What he has is like a fire burning down deep within his belly. When he exhales, his anointed words burns through to man's heart. Past emotion and intellect clearing away the chaff and the unfruitful vines.

This is a Grass Roots movement of Love and Prayer, for every Home and neighborhood. We offer a Correspondent Course to maturate all Christians into Leaders and into a Spiritual SWAT TEAM. These in turn we pray, will encourage, motivate and strengthen others to go out and replicate themselves.

"My people are destroyed for the lack of knowledge: because thou hast rejected knowledge" (Hosea 4:6).

If we receive God's knowledge and refuse to reach out to those who have been rejected then our knowledge is lacking with our own rejection.

People are The Church and *Not* the building!

Just before JESUS ascended into heaven, He promised the Apostles and the first early Church, that He would send a Comforter, one that would bring all things back into their remembrance, and give them power from on high.

As promised the third person of the Godhead, the Holy Ghost did come in Acts chapter two. He gave the early church the power to be witnesses first to their immediate family and closest friends, then out to the entire known world.

The following Eight points, taken from the book of Acts, is what we believe to be the New Emergence of an old way of doing things, the HOME CHURCH.

By the Power of God's Spirit and His love, a Home Church will open in every neighborhood across this great land of ours.

The Home Church is the *Last Line of Defense* against the Spiritual World War III.

CHAPTER ONE

ATTACK ON GOD'S INSTITUTION

The first institutional government was set up by God. From Adam and Eve until JESUS' return, this institution is still GOD'S conduit of blessings to us today, for mankind here on earth. This institution will be called from here on out, as the Marriage Family Structure, one man one woman or it will be called the Home.

Divorce has been raging for decades now. With homosexual marriages on the increase it's even more confusing. When our government promotes fathers not to live with the mothers and rewards them financially. This makes this the most shameful time in our Nation's History. With our Prison system over crowded this causes the single parent to struggle even harder, so without the father, more and more children grow up into, the Criminal System. For our children in the inner cities today, this is the New NORM?

This wild fire is so devastating that our children hardly know anyone or have any peers that have a healthy family structure. It should be, with a loving father and mother with their children living together under one roof. But this is not happening in either the Secular or Christian families. With abortion, drug abuse, physical abuse, adultery, pornography, and homosexuality, no wonder our nation is dying spiritually right before our very eyes. This unrelenting attack marches on, right through our weak defenses, until we are in bondage to our own specific sins. Our Sins, from A to Z, can be found on our cable and satellite providers, as well as on the Internet.

They are designed to feed our souls and emotions the things the god of this world wants you to see and feel. Everything from politics to the lust of your flesh and prides in your life. As the Lord JESUS prolongs his 2nd coming the Sin virus we all have, like cancer will spread throughout our body, soul and spirit. This ultimately will lead us into our own self destruction. If the bondages continues, and a Holy Ghost filled brother or sister does not, come along side and ministers His saving grace and mercy, a lifeless form (made in the image of God) is left to wither away.

In Acts 8:1-3 the families and homes, of the early church were also under attack. House by house, Saul, who was later converted to Apostle Paul, unknowingly he helped spread the gospel. *"Through pains, sufferings, and trials both physically and mentally, are there to show us we need help from outside of ourselves. These are men and women Of God, who are The Wiser and More Mature. Those who teach humility and keep all pride, in check?*

As it began, so it is today, Satan used Paul to attack God's First Institution, house by house, family by family. Back then the family unit was all inclusive.

Each Home passed down from the father to the son unique traditions, and different ways to worship GOD. They knew instinctively, without GOD, they could do nothing.

There are three basic supernatural foundations created in the souls of mankind. They come into play naturally as the family unit becomes more fruitful and multiply. The family was bound together because they needed each other:

1. Economically to work the land or manufacture and distribute their crafts.

2. Socially for their education and healthy family traditions that breed a natural loving environment. Basically, not like today. Back then there were not as many distractions like electronic media, newspapers, magazines etc.

3. They were bound together spiritually, because of a natural, God given, inner desire to worship something greater than them.

Each home and its family tree had a Patriarch or a Matriarch that was known and respected by everyone. They were seen as the wise elder with God's moral values. Sometimes they would sit in the seat of judgment to decide family fights and disputes. These cultures and traditions were passed from the grandfather to the father then to the son. They were taught how to worship God. They new instinctively without God they had no hope.

Who is the wise elder in our modern family structures? Who? is known to be fair and righteous. To be God's moral compass, teaching the family that without the word of God they could do nothing. For without the Lord, the blessings would dry up and there would be no heritage. This is why Satan's attack was then and is now so fierce to break the bonds of the family and destroy their homes.

Is having a legacy and passing along an inheritance nowadays important? I don't think so. Pride, selfishness, materialism, are now the social norms. Like our government. Spend our children's inheritance now and let them make it on their own. Let's eat, drink, travel and be merry and overly indulge in all of the worldly pleasures for tomorrow we die. The devil has done a great job in divide and conquer. He has watered down even the religions of the religious.

The Preaching of The Untruth by the worldly and secular medias, is to intellectualize the vain philosophies of the ways of mankind. To keep men and women sulking in their feelings in the highs and the lows of life. Constantly lusting for pleasures wherever they may be found. The humanistic voices says; "it's okay to be divas and metrosexuals for our young adults". For the older and the wiser among us; They must have power and prestige, they must always look forever young at all cost. Never to look like their real age.

The secular heterosexual married, and The Religious, are building up their individual self esteems so much so they have altered their mindset to say; "I don't need to be married. I'm in bondage to this mate of mine. I can have more fun by myself."

The heterosexual single says; "We don't need to be married, let's just play like it and live together, playing house". While the homosexual say; Let's get married for all the benefits it will bring us".

Confusion, Confusion, Confusion, God is not the author of confusion. (I Corinthians 14:33)

One of the end time signs would be when "Woe unto them that call evil good, and good evil. (Isaiah 5:20) Don't let the supernatural spirits divide and conquer or split your marriage and families, by unbelief and the vanities of this world. (Eccl 4:9-12) There is a promise from God, that there is power in numbers, if the family and friends stay together, and pray together they would not be easily beaten or overpowered.

He knows (Satan) if he can destroy the father or the head of a family, you destroy the home. Destroy the home, you destroy a neighborhood. Destroying a neighborhood destroys a city. Destroy the city, you destroy the state. Destroy the state, you destroy the country. By destroying this country, the United States of America the rest of the world would be easy. Even though weakened, the USA is still the stronghold of the Christian faith.

In the beginning God created the population of the world one family at a time. So one family at a time, Satan is trying to conquer the World.

CHAPTER TWO

THE GOSPEL SENT TO A GENTILES HOME

In the last days, the LORD knew, that the world would be predominantly non-Jewish or Gentiles. That's why in Acts 10, we see that God sends Peter to preach and teach at the home of a Roman soldier who had the rank of Centurion (commanded at least 100 others). He was an Italian named Cornelius. How many times have we gone right past this little nugget of truth?

Right off the bat, God would use somebody outside of the Jewish race to proclaim the Good news of His gospel.

Cornelius and all his family were devout and God fearing people. The WORD also states, "they gave generously to the needy and prayed to GOD always". So to perfect their faith in GOD He sent Peter to teach and anoint them with the power of the Holy Spirit. God always uses people to mature or to perfect the saints for the works of the ministry. Our ministry as a servant means, that those who are called of God are to be servants of others and living sacrifices.

Romans 12:1-2 For the Lord's good pleasure in the world, even the wisdom and the knowledge that you receive from this book, is meant only to mature you only so far. The spiritual leader or the head of the household of the family must sense the urgency of the things happening in the world today. Natural disasters, violence against others, wars, and uncontrollable plagues are Preachers and Signs themselves. As the darkness gets darker the light of the Lord in the saints must shine brighter and brighter in their homes. As violence fills the land, the homes of God's children should be a sanctuary of peace. It should be quite obvious now that the saints of the Lord should be ready for anything that the world, the flesh and the devil may throw at them 24/7/365.

There are no prophecies still to be fulfilled before Jesus' 2nd coming, nothing else needs to happen. Are you ready right now for His 2nd coming? Newsflash, if you think you will be on your best behavior on Sunday morning, because you think that's the only day He will come, you could be sadly mistaken.

Notice how GOD used Cornelius as well, (verse 24) states that he called together his family and closest friends. His home was chosen and sanctified by an angel well in advance of Peter's arrival. The birth of a home church, for the Gentiles came alive that day.

Cornelius, his family and friends no doubt met many times after Peter left, especially now that they have received the power of the Holy Ghost to be witnesses.

The reason we are filled with the Holy Spirit is to take His children to a higher level of understanding of His purposes for their lives. A fresh infilling or what we sometimes call an anointing, shows them and us, God's divine power over evil. Saints (All Christians) need this special anointing to love God, to live by faith without seeing Him visually. We also need to be taught how to walk in the gift of discernment. This helps to know the difference between right and wrong, good and evil. Without this gift from the Lord and His daily presence with us, makes the pressures of this world and its influences, impossible to withstand. This anointing also gave them and us the power to be witnesses to evangelize this sin sick and fallen world.

Through the Lord's mercy and grace is the only way any of us will see God and enter His heaven, and live forever.

We are also given two great commandments (notice not suggestions) in (Matthew 22:36-40) "To LOVE the Lord our God with all, (that's ALL) of your HEART, SOUL and MIND". The second commandment is to Love your neighbor as you LOVE yourself. Because of these two commandments, each and every one of Cornelius' friends and family, I am sure, went back to their own homes and told someone else the GOOD NEWS. And that JESUS was also the GOD of the Gentiles. The Home Churches began to spread with His loving grace, mercy, hope and peace.

At that time Gentiles were not always welcome into the Jewish synagogues for any kind of worship, that's why I believe that the whole house of Cornelius (including his friends) started their own church to worship GOD.

Everyone knows the saved and the unsaved, that this world is in its last days. The field is ripe and ready for harvest. The Ministries of HOME CHURCHES INTERNATIONAL is here to help, to raise you up and to give peace to the weak. To do the work of the ministry that GOD will bless. Let's JUST DO IT!!!

Could have God prepared your heart in advance? Take the spiritual leadership in your family with love.

CHAPTER THREE

YOUR HOUSEHOLD SAVED BY INVITING IN THE WORD OF GOD

In the book of Acts Chapter 16 we see the salvation and the conversion of two different families saved by the power of the living GOD.

First, in verses 14-15 introduces Lydia, who was also a business woman who dealt in purple cloth. The Lord opened her heart to receive the wisdom of His Word, and the power of His mercy and grace. How could she have not shared this Holy revelation with her family? In this fallen world, bad news seems to travel fast, and with the latest technology, information can literally explode around the world in seconds. People now can use camera phones, and send still pictures and videos around the world. Now everyone that has one of these devises can become a worldwide informational broadcaster. So maybe the saints can use this very same technology to spread their own testimonies. That by itself can be a very powerful tool that could be used in the lives of others.

So the disciples Paul and Silas baptized Lydia and her family that day. With her new found faith she asked the disciples to come and stay at her Home for awhile.

Second, in verses 23-34 shows us the next biblical character, set up by the Holy Spirit for our example, in faith building. He is none other than the unnamed Jailer of Paul and Silas. He was literally moved to faith in God by an earthquake. When the jail house doors opened and the chains fell off the prisoners, he decided to take his own Life for fear of his evil superiors. Just think about this for a moment, all this was caused by Paul and Silas praying and singing praises to God. What a miracle!!!

Paul and Silas cried out and stopped the jailer from taking his life, and ministered to him. In short, the Lord saved the jailer and his whole household. That night the jailer took Paul and Silas Home where they baptized him and his family and rejoiced in God.

These two examples of the workings of God are very interesting. In Lydia's case she only needed a gentle nudge to move her heart to faith in Jesus Christ. In the Jailer's case, it might have been over kill, but the Lord used an earthquake to get his attention. In both cases, God's Will was done. Did you also notice that in both cases they brought the Disciples Home?

When you look at some of our old family TV shows like Bonanza, Half Gun Will Travel, Father Knows Best, and even The Little Rascals, it seems like America has lost the concept of being friendly, being hospitable to our neighbors and to our neighborhood. To invite someone outside of the family, a stranger, to stay the night in our own home would be simply out of the question.

The Lord, through the Holy Spirit, opened Lydia's and the Jailer's heart in a way that only He could. In Genesis 6:3 God said "My spirit shall not always strive with man". Every soul of a man has a time and a date stamped on his heart, only known by God's Holy Spirit. Ding! Your time is up! Literally, everything has stopped and frozen in time. You feel a flood of emotions, you can sense in your body, in your soul and in your spirit, something (the presence of the Holy Spirit) like a heavy burden (your sins have been dropped on you) years of bad decisions come into mind. A mental collision between the things done wrong and the things done right in your lifetime. Seconds, turns to minutes, minutes turns to hours, and the weight of all this drama and confusion gets heavier and heavier, and darker and darker. You feel the need to make the decision to live as you were, or to turn around 180 degrees. To accept NOW! Christ's Loving Mercy and Grace, and to live in His Light, is Supernaturally Known to be, the right answer.

In a true conversion there is a supernatural change that takes place in the life of that believer. You want to be enveloped by this new found presence of God.

Not only do you want His presence in your Home, but to merge some way into His very being (God's) into your own. Well, we are God's temple. Please study (1 Corinthians 6:19-21& Luke 17:20-21).

Today our Hearts are enveloped, by our Homes and the things we put in them. Our homes are not only our castles but also our prisons. Within these same homes there are partitions, to separate us, even from our other family members.

The father (if there is one) has his big screen TV room with cable and internet. The wife (if she is one) has the parts of her house that she pours herself into. The children have their rooms with TV, video games and internet games that they can play with others around the world, that keeps them occupied, and out of the way of their parents.

If you are not doing this, do it. Reinstitute family dinners with all in attendance when it's possible. Make this a special time of conversation. Make it "WE" time for family intimacy. The occasional fussing, fighting and complaints should be done some other time!

Do you consider yourself part of a community? How many neighbors do you know intimately? How many people that live and work around you, know that you're a Christian?

The word church, in the original Greek translation means: call out ones, (Does not mean building) people chosen by God into Salvation and to fulfill, his purposes in the world.

If this person is the head of the household, he should view and operate his family like his own personal congregation, (Church) attending to each individual needs, with Love, Prayer and Biblical instruction.

The head of the household by God's Design is the father or the husband. In most cases, nowadays, the man is preoccupied in making a living. If he knows the Lord, he should be leading his family spiritually, if not he automatically unknowingly, passes his headship and the spiritual authority to his wife. Under normal circumstances the wife or the mother instinctively knows the order or the priorities of what it takes to manage the home and the kids.

It wouldn't be the Lord's perfect will, but she is fully capable ***to take the husband's place as the priest, provider and protector.*** Financially she will make sure that the house note, utilities, car payment, with its maintenance schedule being done and paid on time.

Socially, as the mother cooks, feeds and clothes, the children appropriately in the morning, noon and night, even on the weekends. A few other things she might do, is be the transportation manager for schools, sports and church. She will be the maintenance manager for the laundry and the yard work. The educational supervisor for all the homework, assisting with all of the school projects and skits. She will be the Bible teacher, able to handle all of the young ones questions and answer sessions, that may take place anytime 24/7 days a week. Of course when the husband does come home, after working long hours six to seven days a week. She will have plenty of energy left in her tank, to meet and take care of his every whim, which he might imagine in his mind. (Right?)

This is a true statement of most wives and mothers, "if he is not home to do these things, somebody has to do it". I believe no woman wants to take the position of the man. She will, if forced to do so, she'll even be successful for a season. After a few weeks to a few months and she might be able to stay in control. She might even be able to keep her balance, body, soul and spirit. But if it's long and drawn out and there is no hope or no end in sight. If the husband seems to be oblivious to this situation and if he doesn't seem to pick up the changes on her vocal tones, **Her Pot Will Boil Over.** This type of marital relationship is a perfect breeding ground for the breakdown in communication and the Marriage.

The trust they had in each other, has become so weak it is almost non-existent. Constant in fighting, as to who has the final say-so in a matter, is a daily routine. Prayer and marital counseling would be very appropriate at this time. When a man sees his checking, savings and 401K accounts growing with more zeros at the end, it makes it a little easier for him to get what's called tunnel vision. For the believing husband sometimes that's all it will take is for someone from the outside to remind him of Mark 8:36. What profits a man to gain the whole world and to lose his soul. (and family)

PRAISE GOD! Even this, our Lord can redeem. When the family is fully healed and is running smoothly as possible the Lord can and will bless them. He will lead them into His perfect will. It pleases the Lord even more to bring the family His divine favor with men.

Jesus is looking to and fro over the whole earth for vessels, to bring glory to his name and his Father in heaven. These people will be filled and empowered by the Holy Spirit to do even greater things than He has done. He (God) can take a nobody and turn him into somebody that can reach everybody with the Lord's Saving Grace.

Someone in the household must stand up for the Lord. Whoever lifts their hands towards heaven and says, here I am Lord, Use Me! Home Churches International is here to help.

If you are that Called Out One, (the Church) here are seven easy steps to start your family devotions:

In Matthew 18:18-20, is a well known verse of scripture, the teachings I have heard on these two verses have been somewhat shallow, especially if you believe that at the very foundation of the world Christianity, the family started with one man named Adam and one wife Eve that was and is whom the Word of God was sent. Emmanuel (God with us), God commanded the real first family to go forth and be fruitful and multiply and fill the earth. These verses are the real keys of the power for your home, when these keys are understood and applied they will help beat back the mindsets of individualism, selfish prides, and false doctrines.

Jesus here gives us (through the Holy Spirit) the divine permission and authority to do His will. In verses 18, it teaches us the tactics and the spiritual skills of binding and loosing of natural and supernatural things here on earth and in heaven. Jesus taught us in verses 19-20 the power of agreement. When you get at least (two or more) to agree and harmonize in prayer and thought, you can ask God in unity for anything and everything. Ask what so ever you will and it will be done by your Father in heaven. Our teaching in verse 20 maybe somewhat controversial, so here we go. With you and I and one other family member or friend constitutes a fully functional church and even more so because Jesus promised to be in your midst. Jesus also says in Matthew 19:13-15, "permit the little children to come to me and do not forbid them" (you adults and disciples). " For such is the kingdom of heaven" and He laid his hands on them and departed. So if a child at any age can acknowledge Jesus Christ as their Lord and Savior, then they can be used for God's good pleasures like any adult. Because of their childlike faith that is still uncorrupted by the world.

I personally love to have them pray with me in most subjects. God hears and answers the prayers of all His children, grown men and women and the children. There is now no reason for you not to start using the powerful united prayer of agreement. All it takes is for you and one or two others, at any age and Jesus will be right there with you. Go ahead worship, pray and sing praises then get ready for a blessing and His power to reign down on your home.

1. **Serving a Loving Notice.**
   Choose one day and time out of the week you can be committed to. Let it be known to all in your household that this is a good and Godly thing, that's going to happen on this day and this time. On a regular and permanent basis, until further notice.

2. **Expanding Your Prayer Closet.**
   Always be mindful of the leading of the Holy Spirit, if you noticed when Jesus walked and talked with the disciples, He very rarely had long teachings that bored and put people to sleep. They were quick and precise and right to the point. Commandeer one room in the house for at least 15 minutes and no more than one hour.

3. **Anointed to Make it Holy.**
Pray that God will sanctify this time and space thereby making it Holy. A place in which the Holy Spirit can bring conviction, repentance, salvation and exhortation.

4. **You Only Need a Willing and Obedient Heart.**
(The Lord will do the rest) First only invite your entire household to join you in prayer and study, don't let the flesh and the devil give you an excuse why you can't do this. Start with your favorite scripture. God has given us all certain experiences in life, like your testimonies. The Lord has promised that we should not worry about what we should say but in that hour the Holy Spirit himself will give us the words. Just remember in your opening prayer, always use the power that's in the NAME of JESUS, humble and submit yourself and He's in the midst.

5. **Commit to Work Your World.**
Be COMMITTED to this day and time, for this is your PERSONAL CHURCH and mission field. Your world is right there where you live. Starting small is always a good place. Imagine 10,000 square feet around you, that's at least 100 feet out in any direction where you are right now. Think of it like this, you are God's anointed child, each one of us is right in the center of the universe where we stand, like electrons and protons and neutrons revolve around the atom. So does God's salvation and healing powers revolve around you. You have God's peace, when there is no peace. His mercy and grace surrounds you, like that of Moses while being in God's presence. His glory will be upon your face like that also. Depending on what's in the heart of those around spiritually (light or darkness) they will either run to you or run away from you. Remember to literally train all those within and without, of your world, to respect the time that you have scheduled for the family worship. Remind them not to call on

the phone or drop by for a visit, or to temp you with dinner, videos, movies etc. That is meant to throw you off course, so come on, let's be real these things do happen. Don't forget your commitment was to God. We are in a spiritual warfare that is sometimes unseen, stand your ground and take authority over all distractions.

6. **Only Death Can Stop an Ant in His Path.**
An ant will search almost all of his little short life, looking for what he wants in every direction. When he finds it no obstacle will get in his way or stop him from getting the information back to the nest when it is found. When the good news arrives, others are dispatched and a mini freeway is built. This to and fro supply lines moves at a relentless pace that only death can stop. Do not become discouraged if only you are in attendance. It only took one ant to be faithful and diligent searching to find the treasure. We, over our lifetime fought through many obstacles, we weather the storms and found salvation in Jesus. We also found the buried treasures that are in the Living Word of God. So let your light shine and your love and continued faithfulness will draw others in due time by God's Holy Spirit.

7. **Being a ruler over a little.**
God will make you a ruler over much. In Matthew 25:33 Our master in heaven has sown the seeds of the Word of God (The Bible) into our hearts. The seed find the fertile areas and begins to germinate or take root. The first season only produces little fruit, if taken care of and getting well fed, fertilized and watered, it will produce more and more fruit each season.

When the trustworthy man gets his faithful heart tested, God adds a bonus, after he has mastered the little seed for a little area, God will now bless him with even a greater amount of seed and a greater area for him to master over. Accept the fact that God will greatly increase your FAITH because of your obedience and sacrifice. This also allows your knowledge of God's Word, which is in you, to grow, thereby empowering you to do the work of the ministry. Commissioned by Jesus and ordained by the Holy Spirit, not only to save your family but also to reach out to your co-workers, neighbors, neighborhood and on out into the world.

So, tear down the walls inside your home, stretch out your hand to your community, experience the Power and the Blessing of a HOME CHURCH and watch the Lord do many Miracles.

"For where your treasure is, there will your heart be also" (Matthew 6:21)

CHAPTER FOUR

SHARING A MEAL WILL GIVE JOY AND FAVOR WITH MEN

In Acts 2:46-47 we see that the Lord knew that sharing meals from house to house, helps to quiet fears and extinguish preconceived notions of what people think about other people. There is a saying, *"To know me is to love me"*. Men, we always see our neighbors cutting the grass, watering the lawn, or under the hood fixing or doing maintenance to their vehicles, *Right?* So how about investing a few minutes of (planting seed) your life to introduce yourself and maybe compliment them on the great job their doing in maintaining their property. Ask the Lord to give you holy boldness and wisdom in breaking the ice to start a conversation. Sometimes as you drive up and down your neighborhood streets slow down a little and project a quick simple smile, or a nod or wave to acknowledge their existence, and you are being truly glad to see them. It's being a living sacrifice of God's manly (agape) love.

You will find in time that your random acts of kindness, softens their stony hearts. You have allowed yourself to be a vessel for the Lord's goodness to be seen by human eyes. One day as you are walking, jogging or driving, one of these people might stop you or flag you down and initiate a conversation. You might even have a strong inner unction to pray inwardly for them, as they are speaking to you. Always stay humble and go with the flow. You're getting to know them, to love them as the Lord does. Being friendly will draw others to be friends. This allows the individual who feels the tugging of God on their heart, to be more receptive in due season, to the Bible's saving message.

Depending on where you live, there is always that one house or apartment that literally vibrates and thunders with the sound of music. Loud noises, shouts and screams is the norm. The constant foot traffic in and out, back and forth makes you wonder what in the world goes on over there. Under normal circumstances children and adults stay away from these kinds of situations. They usually become magnets for the aints (unbelievers) of darkness with all its variances.

Your home, with its HOME CHURCH (where two or more saints can gather) should become the community safe haven, where spiritual rest and peace can be found. Don't be surprised when one of your neighbors, when you least expect it, ask you sincerely from their heart for advice to a moral dilemma they find themselves in. Oh, what an opportunity.

I am not saying go out and have big neighborhood barbecues, but what I am saying, in the morning sometimes, invite your neighbor over for coffee or share a cup over the fence in the back or front yard. For women to come together to share tea and crumpets is a great way to get to know each other.

Men are good at gathering around sporting events. We eat dips and chips and hot wings sharing knowledge of our favorite team. When we're hollering and yelling at our big screens for or against our teams, we are having fun getting to know our fellow brethren in couch potatoism, for a season or two. The real bottom line is all of this male and female fellowship is that the (breaking of bread) consumption of good food and drink is a very intimate thing to do with one another. The physical union in a relationship (between the married couples of course) is the only other thing two people can do that brings more peace and a sense of well being than sharing a meal together.

The point is, to be bold in your faith in Jesus Christ, You will be lead as to what, when, where and how to share our Savior Jesus. When you study and do God's Word, He blesses you with wisdom and special favor.

"Devote yourselves to prayer, being watchful and thankful. And pray for us, too, that God may open a door for our message so that we may proclaim the mystery of Christ, for which I am in chains. Pray that I may proclaim it clearly, as I should. Be wise in the way you act toward outsiders; make the most of every opportunity. Let your conversation be always full of grace, seasoned with salt, so that you may know how to answer everyone". Colossians 4:2-6 (NIV)

"Do your best to present yourself to God as one approved, a workman who does not need to be ashamed and who correctly handles the word of truth". 2 Timothy 2:15 (NIV)

CHAPTER FIVE

THE BIBLICAL PRIORITIES AND OCCUPYING UNTIL HE COMES

In order to affect the world, we must not be religious but first get our minds and our homes, in order before the Lord. Our God is not the author of confusion or disorder (1 Corinthians 14:33). The Saints of God, we his children, lives life of turmoil, pains and sufferings, because we do not have a goal or a vision for our daily living. (Proverbs 29:18) "Without a vision the people perish". We reap what we sow or we harvest nothing because we sow nothing. If we don't prioritize the who, what, when and where, this means that our daily choices are made on whims and foolish prayers. If you have ever felt like a dog chasing his own tail, you know exactly what I'm talking about. As you mature into God's word, you will find that there are two tracks, or paths that He uses to grow his children, from the babies milk of the bible, to the rich chunky meat of His word. The names of these tracks or paths of life are:

1. God's Perfect Will
2. God's Permissive Will

The definition of the word "will" is strong and fixed purpose and determination. The word "permissive" is defined as allowing freedom; tolerate of behavior or practices disapproved by others; indulgent; lenient.

Let not your heart be troubled because 99% of us spend time on this physiological merry-go-round depending on the subjects and the weaknesses of our flesh. We can get off and back on, to this spiritual contraption hundreds of times in our lifetime. Maybe it's time to fast and pray, asking the Lord what is His vision and purpose for you. Look into the nook and crannies of your heart. I believe they have always been there under the boxes of discouragement, in the bags of old clothes of pain and bitterness. Look way down deep into the back of the closet where the secret things lie, in the corners and the cracks, behind the walls of sexual sins. There we hide our bondages, addictions, abuses, curses and etc.

Usually, your purpose has been planted by God himself when we were younger and somewhat innocent, when you find your purpose dust it off, shine it up and make short consistent obtainable goals. Prioritize every action, every day. A "To Do List" sometimes works very well to start. If you continue as you are, you will stop your spiritual growth. Anything that stops growing becomes stagnant; this is when a life of confusion and disorders reestablishes themselves.

In James 1:8 basically teaches that a man and woman that gets stuck between two choices, is not only double minded but is also mentally unstable in all the things that he does. Please don't harden your heart today. If you sense the tug of God's Holy Spirit, this proves that you are a free moral creature, able to choose between right and wrong. Don't let God just be tolerant of your behavior (permissive will), choose the blessed purpose that he has for you, choose life. By the way, not to make a choice today, is a choice.

Every time you willfully surrender, your will to the Lord's perfect will, you will experience the peace of His presence. He causes your mind and emotions to be at rest, like a spiritual Jacuzzi that soothes every part of your body, soul and spirit. You have casted your every cares and burdens onto Jesus. He cares for you (Matthew 11:28-30) & (1 Peter 5:6-7). His perfect will and promise for you is eternally strong and fixed, because of His unconditional love for you. It will be easy to be yoked, or bonded (married) to Him. Because your relationship with your Lord and Savior is so precious, that the burden to be obedient in His word, is light.

The Biblical Priorities and Spiritual Order in Life are:

1. To love the Lord your God with all your heart, with all your mind, with all your soul and with all your strength and His word.

    A. Pray, study, fellowship, and serve and be a giver are commands.
    B. Fasting as led, gives Supernatural Power and Faith to Overcome.

2. Be the spiritual leader in your family.

    A. If married this should be the man.
    B. He should love his wife as Christ loves the church.
    C. He should be the Priest, Pastor, Provider and Protector of the family.

3. Love His children.

    A. Teach them the scriptures, when you walk along the road, write them on the doorpost, hang them on the walls.
    B. Lead by example. As much as you possibly can, live each day like Jesus is right there beside you, leading you in the paths of righteousness.

4. On your job do all things as onto the Lord.

    A. Let your light shine that men might see your good works and glorify God.

5. Minister to all others outside your home, with godly wisdom.

   A. Be bold as led by the Holy Spirit with all humility.
   B. Be sure that there is no lack from #1 thru #6.

6. Political and Social Activism is a good thing.

   A. Get active in the cities chamber of commerce or PTA or start a neighborhood watch program etc.
   B. Attend school board meetings.
   C. Know your local state and federal issues, being loyal to one particular party is dangerous, your vote is a vow that you support that candidate or issue.
   D. Vote for candidates that have the highest moral value in light of God's word.
   E. Diligently check his or her voting record (Google it).
   F. Seek out the facts not the feelings and never make an emotional decision.

Paul the Apostle kept nothing back that was profitable or helpful as it says in Acts 20:19-21. Through many tears and temptations the testing of his faith, Paul fought on through many plots, though many traps were set. Today I call this spiritual resistance, The **"divide and conquer technique"** of Christianity. This **waters down our Doctrine** into many religions and denominations. Major **offensive sins** are attacking our country and it's constitution through all medias and all of our institutes of education from preschool to college.

He (Paul) overcame because he was compelled and empowered by God's Spirit to preach and teach the word publicly from house to house. Even then the Jews and Gentiles were so corrupt, their sins had to be exposed by the light of God's word. Just like now, the exposure should be on a one on one individual basis. Paul taught repentance and faith toward our Lord Jesus Christ.

This too is still our mission, if you look back on the Biblical order of things (1 thru 6) you can see our enemy. Our own flesh and the Devil could have and will set traps and plots for us today. Most plots and traps, stumbling or flat out spiritual warfare are still in today's ministries and churches. Their Ministers must not just preach against sin but also work with the lack of finances. And this failing economy just made things worse, faster.

Let's go back to a simpler time, about 150 years ago. The family knew the importance of owning land. They had to grow their own food, the family farm is where everybody grew up, including the extended family, the aunts, uncles and cousins. The more children you had, the more farm hands you had. The larger the family the more you were considered to be, a very blessed man and wife. Because you had many more hands to work. The more hands you had, the more land you could grow more various kinds of crops. You also had farm animals to raise, to take to the market for a financial gain. This was a booming time for the early America. The immigrants from Europe were still pouring in by the thousands. Mostly Christian Protestants, Catholics, Jews and Gentiles, a melting pot of all kinds of people, knowing and serving the one true God.

The common prayer of all was something like this, "Lord, please bless our health and our hands and grant us a new start in this fruitful land." The Lord did bless them, they worked before sun up to sundown they all ate at least breakfast and dinner together (no refrigeration) and offered up prayers of Thanksgiving for everything they had.

As more and more people move into a rural America, large events took place several times a year. The bartering system was well in place. The families that lived relatively close to one another, swapped goods with each other for all kinds of fruits and vegetables, meats, eggs, large and small animals all without little or no money. Value for value, sometimes the newcomers and even the current residences need new barns or houses, home editions and even fencing.

I believe that there is a God given natural understanding that's deep and has been planted very deep into our souls and spirits. That humanity was created to need each other. These people would come together mostly volunteering their time to complete these large constructions in a timely manner before the rains. They automatically knew that they had to help each other, for the time would surely come, that their family would need their communities to help in the future.

Usually sometimes around harvest time the farming community would come together and fellowship, they would eat, drink and be merry and even took time to worship God and give thanks for their fruitful season and the next. They all had to live daily for the Lord because he was at the center of everything that they called life.

When the railway system moved in, the world literally got smaller and smaller. Small towns were built near the train tracks. In these towns the first building was usually the largest, it was the church house, it was not only to worship God and to have weddings. The church also doubled as a community center, for everything from public meetings, rallies and even as a court house. Hotels and apartments had to be built for the business travelers. The people that would be working in these towns that soon became cities. These city folks built the first suburbs just right outside of town. The early roots and foundations of America were truly blessed by the hand of God. Mostly all of the colleges (including the Ivy Leagues) were built on the premise that all graduate students mandatorily had to have a degree in Theology. For this new nation to stand, to keep its freedoms, knowing its God that blessed this country was paramount.

In the early 1900's America was a superpower, with no enemies for awhile. With great wealth and prosperity, the elect of our country succumbed to the love of money. The demonic spirits of greed and power went to work, not just in the United States of America but also in Europe for it to was being resurrected.

Pressing on, we are going to fast forward through World War I and World War II, the Korean War, the Cold War, Vietnam and now the war in the Middle East. All because of the demonic spirits of greed, power, pride and lust.

A Spiritual Nuclear Bomb that went off in the late 1960's without making a sound. Ground zero was a dairy farm in a small town of Bethel, (means; House of God) in the state of New York, it was called Woodstock. For those who have spiritual eyes to see, Satan exposed his major plot to destroy God's plan for mankind. Right out of the book of Genesis 28:17-19 is the place that Jacob named for meeting the Lord and his Angels. He named that place Bethel meaning house of God. We know now that we, the Saints or the Christians are the temples for the Holy Spirit to live within. The whole premise of this book is how Christians should turn their homes into houses of God. Those three days in August 1969, America was infected with a large dose of the sin virus.

Slowly and but surely **Desensitized** our moral values even more. In some form right now, to this day, just about every home in America has experienced some form of a watered down, faithless, and powerless religion. So that some Christians and Unbelievers are **virtually indistinguishable.**

This was the beginning of the most deadly destruction, ever so slowly for the souls of men in all eternity. World War III is a full on fight to the death in the spiritual realm. Pandora's box was open and millions of spirits were unleashed upon America. The Woodstock festival in the town of Bethel is where all this began. The main focus of our enemy was the sex, the drugs and rock and roll and many other forms of indecency. With the willing media recording and broadcasting live news clips in Living Color. Hours upon hours, visuals of signs that read "Make love not War, Burn Bras, Legalize Pot".

The evil spirits that day, began its oppression to possession of the young souls and minds that attended. The possession of some of those people that day, became the Hippies and the Tie Dye t-shirts became the "Liberal Anything Goes Generation". The spiritual darkness of that generation is still alive today, they now wear suits and ties and hold high positions of power on Main Street, Wall Street, Hollywood, Local, State and Federal positions.

That mindset is still in our U.S. Congress, Senate, Supreme Court and all the way up to the White House itself. Yes, Woodstock was a sneak attack right when this country was the most open and vulnerable to the television. They broadcasted to our businesses, organizations, schools and even our homes. America loved its family programming, showing some wholesome depiction of God and Country and the victories of past wars. The modern life with the father as the head and a loving wife at his side, and a hand full of obedient children. We watched and absorbed everything, right in our living rooms on a nightly basis. We viewed the righting of wrongs done during the civil rights movement. Newborn babies coming into this world at a record pace. Everybody was happy for a season.

Question? Do you walk in logic and can filter the past, present and maybe even the future events with good old fashion common sense? I pray that you can, because my next question could really expose yourself to yourself, or you may have your head stuck in the sand and **not in reality**. Here is a hint, **the answer is Spiritual.**

Are all things better today in the United States of America than in the 1960's. A resounding **"NO"** is the right answer.

Like in Luke 19:11-27 which says v11 *"And as they heard these things, he added and spake a parable, because he was nigh to Jerusalem, and because they thought that the kingdom of God should immediately appear.* v12 *He said therefore, A certain nobleman went into a far country* **(JESUS' Death & Now King of Heaven & Earth)** *to receive for himself a kingdom, and to return.* v13. *And he called his ten servants, and delivered them ten pounds, and said unto them, Occupy till I come.* v14. *But his citizens hated him, and sent a message after him, saying, We will not have this man to reign over us.* v15. *And it came to pass, that when he was returned, having received the kingdom,* **(JESUS' 2nd Coming)** *then he commanded these servants to be called unto him, to whom he had given the money, that he might know how much every man had gained by trading.* v16. *Then came the first, saying, Lord, thy pound hath gained ten pounds.* v17. *And he said unto him, Well, thou good servant: because thou has been faithful in a very little, have thou authority over ten cities.* v18. *And the second came, saying, Lord thy* *pound hath gained five pounds.* v19. *And he said likewise to him, Be thou also over five cities.*

v20. *And another came, saying, Lord, behold, hear is thy pound, which I have kept laid up in a napkin:* v21. *For I have feared thee, because thou art an* **(stern)** *austere man: thou takest up that thou layedst not down, and reapest that thou didst not sow.* v22. *And he saith unto him, Out of thine own mouth will I judge thee, thou wicked servant. Thou knewest that I was an austere man, taking up that I laid not down, and reaping that I did not sow:* v23. *Wherefore then gavest not thou my money into the bank, that at my coming I might have required mine own with* **(interest***) usury?* v24. *And he said unto them that stood by, Take from him the pound, and give it to him that hath ten pounds.* v25. *(And they said unto him, Lord, he hath ten pounds.)* v26. *For I say unto you, That unto everyone which hath shall be given; and from him that hath not, even that he hath shall be taken away from him.* v27. *But those mine enemies, which would not that I should reign over them, bring hither, and slay them before me".*

We were given a little from God's merciful hands, from 13 colonies, to us being the lone superpower on earth. We were slowly but now faster and faster turning our back on our creator and the giver of life, through whom all blessings flow. **(Is it because some believe that the Word of God which is Lord Jesus is austere or to stern with us)**

In this parable the meaning is that Jesus Christ is the man of noble birth. Before he went to a far distant country (heaven) to be made king over his kingdom. He called or chosen certain servants that he might bless with a certain amount of riches. When he would return he would check on them. In the next phrase, Jesus gives a command that is **least taught** and **hardly ever obeyed** by all of Christendom all around the world.

In essence the command was to **occupy**, buy, sell, do business and put his money to work, so whatsoever the amount. In keeping with the priority set forth in this chapter (1 thru 6), I believe within any country of the world, the Saints, God's children should be a majority owner in all things, wealth and things that have a value.

30 | *The Return of God's Power "In Your Home"*

The word occupy is translated from the word in Hebrew (machoz or maw-khoze) which means to gain by trade or hold a land or position.

Before I go any further you must remember, (I Timothy 6: 10) it is the love of money that is the root of all evil. Money is a tool, a crop or a seed. I believe Jesus was teaching us on a very base level something I learned in Economics 101. In business we must expand, maintain, and protect our interest if we are to be successful. In (Proverbs 13:22) *"A good man leaveth an inheritance to his children's children: and the wealth of the sinner is laid up for the just".*

For a moment let's go back to Luke 19: 14-27, many of the kings servants hated him and didn't want him to rule over them. In the end when he came back the kings enemies was slain before him. The disobedient servant that received or was blessed by the King's valuables, did absolutely nothing with them, while he was gone a long time. (See the parallel parable in Matthew 25: 14-30). And suffered a great lost. We must also ponder this, God's thoughts are not our thoughts, and His ways are not our ways. In verses (Luke 19:16-19) the King of Kings, Jesus blessed two good servants with money, they were so obedient in ruling over money that they each received multiple cities in return for them to rule over. Saints, whatever the Lord has blessed you with, rule over It, and don't let It rule over you. No matter how small, you must be consistently faithful. Be obedient to all of what God has commanded in His word. We will reap a reward that is unmatched, and incomprehensible. But we must remember He is still watching how we will rule over the more.

The Lord has given us all salvation and the good news of the gospel, the hope of heaven. We must tell others and **expand** it, we're commanded to grow by reading, studying, to be approved of God by **maintaining** it. We need to be filled by the Holy Ghost for a discerning heart and have an answer why our hope is in the gospel to **protect** it. Only then when we are judged, we will be rewarded for still **cccupying** and gaining by trading **until He comes**. Maybe He'll give us planets next.

"And they continued steadfastly in the apostles doctrine and fellowship, and in breaking of bread, and in prayers" (Acts 2:42). *"Praising God, and having favor with all the people. And the Lord added to the church daily such as should be saved".* (Acts 2: 47)

So now you see that it is very profitable, beneficial and helpful for us to belong to a Home Church, all relationships are more intimate because it is a smaller environment, where Godly emotions, feeling and Godly discernment can flourish. On a individual basis we must always stay humble and maintain a teachable spirit. Accountability is automatic because of close relationships someone will see you falling before you fall. After you get to know better your neighbors, your in-laws your out-laws and learn to love them unconditionally the way Christ does, it will be very hard not to share His goodness from house to house the way Paul did.

CHAPTER SIX

APOSTLE PAUL'S STAND AGAINST FALSE TEACHING AND STARTS A HOME CHURCH

In Acts 28:30-31 Paul the Apostle rented a house for two years right in the middle of Rome, while under house arrest. "There he preached and taught the kingdom of God with all confidence. No man hindering or forbidding him. He received all that came to him". Here we see Paul's burning desire to preach and teach God's saving knowledge to the gentiles of Rome.

Today modern man still has a burning desire, it just happens to be for more of the material things of this world. The right clothes and colors that look best with his complexion that goes along with the four seasons of the year. The trophy wife, the right house, the right car proves where one resides on the social economic ladder. Jesus said, **"Come just as you are"**, your outward appearance doesn't matter, God looks at the heart. Oh! How blessed we are, and spoiled too, only in America Christians think this way.

These things are not totally all bad in and of themselves, only if these things are your only desires. The material blessings we have should only be a by- product of our faith in God . I have found, or should I say God has proven to me, that when I give my Tithes FAITHFULLY, God can bless the 90%, more than if I had kept the whole 100%. It just is a SUPERNATURAL fact, that when a man gives the first fruits of his income to God, by FAITH, CHEERFULLY pride and materialism are NOT a part of one's character.

Some people will not open their homes for fear of damage or theft. Be sure to use wisdom in things you may leave out, but remember there is no fear in love, because perfect love casts out fear (1 John 4:18).

When you minister God's Word in a home, it seems to be a less threatening atmosphere. The true personalities and the character of people, expose themselves. We see their weaknesses as well as their strengths. If we look deep enough we can discern their gifts and their differences given by God to fulfill His purposes, and His Will for the Church.

I know you just wanted a little privacy. Ok, let's look at this word "privacy" avoidance of notice, a place of seclusion, secrecy. Looks to me like the Body of Christ, has done this long enough. Here we are the salt of the earth, having the power to lay hands on the sick, able to bind the enemies of our faith. With all of God's gifts and promises at our disposal, we can only find enough strength, to put on a big smile and hide out, in the back of our churches on Sundays. This should not be so.

When you go to a church, remember whatever you look for, most of the time you will find. If you look for negatives you'll see negatives. We should always give God's people, our brothers and sisters the benefit without doubt, while visiting seek for God and his word. We must have His unconditional love in our heart, mind and spirit to discern properly. Therefore when you first enter, you should sense the presence of Jesus and the Holy Ghost's loving anointing, upon that place. If not be careful and guard your heart, and test the spirits by the spirits. (I John 4:1-3) *Beloved, believe not every spirit, but try the spirits whether they are of God: because many false prophets are gone out into the world. v2. Hereby know ye the Spirit of God: Every spirit that confesseth that Jesus Christ is come in the flesh is of God. v3. And every spirit that confesseth not that Jesus Christ is come in the flesh is not of God: and this is that spirit of antichrist, whereof ye have heard that it should come; and even now already is it in the world.*

Until you find a Pastor/Teacher and he must have both of these gifts, it's okay to feed yourself and your family at home. The tradition nowadays is to break up the families into the nursery and children's church, the teen fellowship, young adults and singles. Given what I know of history I don't think that's very healthy. I know this to, is controversial but this is the very same philosophy that has permeated our minds. It also has broken the biblical value and morals in the traditional family unit, This is socialism that came from our national schooling system. I think if bible study works at the home, without breaking up the family, why should we, do it at our churches. The so called peer pressure in our young ones life, the gang banging in our older ones would cease to exist. The familiar love they would have for one another would cause more talking and sharing, and communicating from the heart. It would create an eternal bond. Families that grow up like this can make it through anything with the Lord's help. The gates of Hell itself would never prevail against them. For every father and single mom that is reading this book, God had taken away your excuses for not serving the Lord.

Now no one, for the most part can say to themselves, this Sunday we can't go to church because:

- It's too far.
- Those people don't like us.
- That church is full of hypocrites.
- It's too hot or it's too cold.
- It's raining out there.
- I'm too old and tired.
- I'm too young to die I just want to have some fun first.
- All they want is my money, etc.

Throughout the pages of this book you will have learned that in these last days there will be no excuses accepted. Referring to when the eternal judgment happens. Let's look at a few verses pertaining to the last day Saints and their excuses.

"Now the Spirit speaketh expressly, that in the latter times some shall depart from the faith, giving heed to seducing spirits, and doctrines of devils" (I Timothy 4:1). The saints of God (His children) will leave their faith in the latter times because of the love of money and all forms of material lusts and every kind of sexual deviance you can imagine. There are specific and certain kinds of demonic spirits that attack us in our weaknesses.

Matthew 7:21-23." *Not everyone that saith unto me, Lord, Lord, shall enter into the kingdom of heaven; but he that doeth the will of my Father which is in heaven. v22. Many will say to me in that day, Lord, Lord, have we not prophesied in thy name? and in thy name have cast out devils? And in thy name done many wonderful works? v23. And then will I profess unto them, I never knew you: depart from me, ye that work iniquity".* This is very clear that there are Christians that can fool their friends and family and sometimes fool their Pastors. When judgment time comes, you'll find that you never fooled the Lord, because He looks on your heart.

2 Thessalonians 2:1-3. *"Now we beseech you, brethren, by the coming of our Lord Jesus Christ, and by our gathering together unto him. v2. That ye be not soon shaken in mind, or be troubled neither by spirit, nor by word, nor by letter as from us, as that the day of Christ is at hand. v3. Let no man deceive you by any means: for that day shall not come, except there come a falling away first, and that man of sin be revealed, the son of perdition".*

Here the Christians are being taught that before the coming of our Lord Jesus Christ, don't become disturbed or lose your spiritual composure or allow fear to set in. There will be false reports and letters that Jesus has already came and left you behind.

I'm telling you now that this wicked world, is coming to an end. But don't be deceived Saints, there are two signs you should be watching for. First there is an apostasy, a falling away from the churches, I believe that for some time now this sinful rebellion has already begun. The Second thing happening, is The Man of Sin, the Antichrist False Messiah, his spirit will be accepted. The backslidden Christian and the people of the world will open their hearts and their souls to him. He will be proclaiming himself as God, and will want to be worshipped. Matthew 24:10-12. *And then shall many be offended, and shall betray one another, and shall hate one another.* v11. *And many false prophets shall rise, and shall deceive many.* v12. *And because iniquity shall abound, the love of many shall wax cold.*

THE SIGNS OF THE LAST DAYS

Today's Agnostics, Unbelievers, the Religions and the Christians alike can see we are at the end of the ages. As we all watch with our own eyes, we see humanity and creations spiraling downward out of control. Soon this toilet bowl must flush. The war in Iraq and Afghanistan, the fighting and the murders in Africa. North and South Korea are about to explode. Earthquakes, tsunamis, tornadoes, giant sink holes in the earth, mud slides and floods. Volcanoes, global cooling or global warming, you take your pick, all these prove that creation is sick of the Sins of Mankind. Ever heard of these? HIV, STD's, H1N1, Superbugs resistant to known antibiotics, famines and other diseases are on their way back. Like polio and whooping coughs.

Being Easily Offended

Even though we stumble and trip over all of the blessings of God, we have become a nation of whining litigious cry babies. If a person has a thought, real or imagine, what is right or wrong, legal or illegal, the fact of common sense can be thrown out the window. It's all about the feelings, what that person feels at the time, is the only thing that matters. Lawsuits between friends, family, co-workers and even church members are on the rise.

I have heard it said that Christianity in the United States is not numerically growing with brand new believers in our churches, but people are church hopping or pop corning, because these people wear their Emotions on their sleeves.

They pop in a new ministry that teaches a good word or not, being an excellent Pastor of a loving church or not, is not the issue. They're looking to be offended, so they can pop out without guilt or shame. They mostly don't want accountability. They say, "How dare someone correct us and teach us how to grow through our trials and tribulations. Who do they think they are?" they would say. "They probably want us to study the bible and do what it says, like give 10% of our money".

These are the things that nomadic type Christians do and say. Then they say, "Let's go find a church, where we can just sit, way in the back where nobody will notice. God knows that we are trying to be good people, after all being in Church every Sunday morning is the most important thing, Right Dear?"

Is this what you think about God's word and His children? The enemy doesn't manipulate our bodies against us necessarily, because it has its own appetites and is a slave to whatever is in control. He can't touch our spirit because it's always tuned into the Lord's Will for our lives. Our Spirit always tries to Lead our Body and Soul, to do what is right.

The enemy's number one place to attack us, is in our eternal soul/emotions. He is the master at manipulating the weak spots in our character. All in the spiritual realm he is able, to scan the hearts and mind of those around us. Exposing our prides and fleshly lust, as he probes and pushes buttons, we began to display those certain looks. With our eyes we project what the Devils-schemes are, for us in that moment.

The weirdest thing in moments like these are that 85% to 95% of the spiritually mature, all the way to the ignorant, aren't able to discern when this is happening. Our tongues flutter to maintain supremacy. The enemy's thoughts, which our now our thoughts finds us using words of false humility towards one another.

What may have started as a conversation, he'll do whatever it takes to turn up the heat and the volume. He wants an emotional outburst in words and deeds. Wanting us to offend and hurt mentally and to turning it physical is always the desired reaction. Please, please, please or verily, verily, verily I say unto to my brother and sister in Christ Jesus our Lord, controlling our soulish emotions with its prides, is God's Perfect Will for us.

Deception and Betrayal of Each Other

Very slowly, over the last 100 years or so, we have become less and less Godly (biblically deceived), as a nation. There is a Master Mind behind it all, to desensitize our minds about our own values. There is a game you can play called Jenga, it's about 40 rectangle blocks of wood, one inch square by four inches long. They are so perfectly stacked it becomes a small wooden tower about 12 inches high. The object of this game is for two people, in turn to slowly remove one block at a time. In a short while the tower begins to wobble and rock to and fro, as more and more blocks are removed. The last person to move or even touch the last block in the tower to make it fall is the loser.

This is exactly how the Fallen Angels used the many false prophets that are in these last days. They have turned the American dream (the having of everything you want, while still being young) into a nightmare. This recent economic down turn that started in 2008, with people losing jobs and homes, is still happening now. The American Dream is now a part of our philosophy and culture. If it takes both parents to obtain this goal, then so be it.

Over the years, this way of thinking, is just warmed over and repackaged greed. Our welfare system is a scheme from the darkness as well. It teaches without saying, to the poorest young men and women among us, that there are good consequences to sex and promiscuity. If the two of you have made a baby, no problem. The government will take care of everything, but all of you daddy's, you can't live in the same home to raise, provide and protect your children. Daddy's if you have any guilt or shame about all this, **get over it!** Go have fun, find some other poor fatherless little girl and make more babies. We'll take care (the government's national welfare system) of them all.

Small home churches, in these scenarios can be a beacon of light and hope in the middle of these neighborhoods. Today, men and women are becoming more and more selfish. The various forms of lust and greed or the keeping up with the Joneses have become an art form and a subculture unto itself. All ages the young and old, across the races, religions, even in mainstream Christianity, we now all have to have the latest and greatest cell phones, cars and computers. We need designer shoes, clothes and purses, no wonder the rest of the world laughs at us and hates us, because they want to be like us. (with tongue and cheek)

They watch us as the demonic spirits amplify it all through television, movies and the internet. I have traveled the world and in my conversations with the people, they think all American Women are shopaholics or closet lesbian and our Men are cowboys or closet homosexuals.

Deceptions and betrayals in some form or another happens in every second throughout our day, they are so numerous to contemplate or even verbalize. These two have become just the way we do things. In Romans 1:21 *Because that, when they knew God, they glorified him not as God, neither were thankful; but became vain in their imaginations, and their foolish heart was darkened* (to get things done).

From these unseen realms of darkness there is one more strategy implemented in our nation, and there is a good sign of repealing this. It is the sacrificial killing of our babies for birth control and profit. If this is not bad enough for you, look at this undeniable fact how Satan has done this. He has put these killing centers (abortion clinics for Planned Parenthood), in the middle or on the edges of our poorest and crime ridden counties, cities and neighborhoods all across America. I know that millions of these young girls were raped and forced into having these abortions.

I know that many of these were paid for by the parents or the boy friend/father. I also know that all of these participants have scared consciences. Over the years the "what if" mind games, we played within ourselves, kept us wounded and bitter. But God, has enough mercy and grace to cover and forgive (1 Peter 4:8 & Romans 5:20) a multitude of sins.

But for the others could this evil plan and law be a strategy or a silent attack to wipe out or to hinder the growth of certain races of people? This wickedness alone grieves the heart of God. God will judge those to Hell, for Murdering (Galatians 5:21) the Lives, of those he has given it to.

Hating Each Other

Hate is defined as having a strong dislike or ill will for, loath or to despise. To hate is one of the strongest emotions a man can have. It also has at least two other evil twins their names are Covet and Pride. In this evil family of emotions there is a stepbrother that makes the other three look like cub scouts. He is called Murder, this gang of four, always run together, as they play in the lives, of those that let them in.

Hate goes back all the way to Cain and Abel. Because of pride Cain thought that God should have taken the sacrificial work of his hands. In hate, he rather take the life of another human, than a creature as the Lord has commanded. This is still the mindset of millions on earth. Some think if they gave money, donate homes, buildings and lands that this would please the Lord and buy themselves salvation, and get their ticket to heaven. Nothing like that could be further, from the truth, more than likely that kind of thinking, would send you to the other place, under the volcanoes.

Over the years, millions of people hated and died because:

- People hated each other because someone has what they want and can't have it now, like beauty and being handsome.
- People hated each other because they want fame and power, fast cars, rings, watches, high fashion clothing, a trophy wife or girlfriend.
- People hated each other for gold and lands.
- People hated each other because of successes in their businesses.
- People hated each other for the need of water.
- People hated each other because you remind them of someone else.

- People hated each other because of a certain outward look and just different than you.
- People hated each other because they have different Ideologies or religion.

But because of wickedness in our flesh we can choose to hate, almost anything we want. Your family's culture and the way you've been raised, has a lot to do with the way you think and process information. Most pediatric doctors and psychiatrist agree that when you are around seven years old, 60% to 70% of the foundation of your character has been built.

Sins and Iniquities on the Increase

Every movie made in Hollywood and its surrounding areas (for the most part), are little visual representations of depths in which a man's mind can sink. We spend billions of dollars to amuse ourselves. Whenever we feel the need to escape from the pressures of reality, we jump into our cars, and go to the nearest movie house with a drink and a bag of popcorn, we sit in plush chairs in a dark room. Being filled with excitement, we anxiously await the start of this chosen movie. About halfway into the movie, our breath deepens and our heart pumps just a little faster. Thundering sounds and the flashing of the lights and the colors begins to over stimulate us. They are showing gigantic depictions of things that we would never do or allow ourselves to be around in real life Or Would We?

These so called Art Forms are the new demonic spiritual preachers that are widely accepted in our homes. While allowing, the back ground noise from the television, radio and the internet we subconsciously consume this stuff that fills our minds with everything under the sun 12 to 16 hours per day.

My Father used to say "garbage in, garbage out, you are, what you eat". Never have words rung so true. No wonder alcohol, drug abuse legal and illegal, mental illnesses, heart attacks and suicides are on the increase, it's because of our fast paced world were in.

We all still can do, everything we want to do, things just need to move even faster, Don't they? Are we all becoming adrenaline junkies? As we daily fill ourselves with all of the world's issues and problems, were forced to take time to Rest our Physical Bodies. *That's a shame; maybe all I need is a pill or an energy drink.* Now on the weekends we are temporarily rested and at peace and at a place of quietness ready to get back to our mundane, repetitive realities. On Sunday mornings we soon get bored because things are moving to slow. You have no social life, because those people are crazy out there. So we sit down and get a half gallon of our favorite ice cream and turn on the TV news and every other media retrieving device, to get back to our place of peace and the comfort of NOISE. *Yes, good for nothing noise; an idle mind is the devil's workshop.*

Here's another saying "The movies, videos, video games and the like, teaches cursing, and violence". So we who live in the larger cities curse and do violence to one another. What else is there to do when you're young, strong and penniless? Well you have sex, make babies, do drugs, with murder mayhem around you, this is what you do. What is there to stop them? Who and what is offering them any alternatives? Let's relearn about the real Love, the real Peace and the Real Hope that's found only in The Word of God.

I believe some are becoming tired of stepping on each other, to get higher. The preachers of sin and materialism take their jobs very seriously. In these latter days sins against God will increase, because sin is pleasurable (2 Timothy 3:4). Agree with me in prayer for the Lord's Holy Boldness, mixed with the Saving Grace of Jesus Christ, that we would truly live for CHRIST in our homes first. Then take this Spiritual Warfare to the streets, winning one soul at a time.

Paul and Barnabas exposing lies and false teaching
Acts 15:24-29

Forasmuch as we have heard, that certain which went out from us have troubled you with words, subverting your souls, saying, Ye must be circumcised, and keep the law: to whom we gave no such commandment:

v25. *It seemed good unto us, being assembled with one accord, to send chosen men unto you with our beloved Barnabas and Paul. v26. Men that have hazarded their lives for the name of our Lord Jesus Christ. v27. We have sent therefore Judas and Silas, who shall also tell you the same things by mouth.*

v28. *For it seemed good to the Holy Ghost, and to us, to lay upon you no greater burden than these necessary things; 29. That ye abstain from meats offered to idols, and from blood, and from things strangled, and from fornication: from which if ye keep yourselves, ye shall do well. Fare ye well.*

The Love of Many Growing Cold

Today, some of our churches teach the will of it's congregation, bringing big name preachers to preach. Spending thousands of dollars for musical artist, to excite the people and ministers. If the pastor is a feeling and emotional oriented person, his Board of Directors more than likely also will be feeling oriented. But if the Pastor and the Board of Directors has their fingers on the pulse of the people and are people pleasers. When does the Will of God and the Leading of the Holy Spirit come into play in this drama? When they purchase media airtime, everything and everybody has to look just right. The right kind of people and the right kind of faces, must be in the right chairs and the right row. All of this planning has to be timed to the second, for the perfect 50 minute time of worship. So let's see the bulletin.

In the Mega Church
The Order of Service:

- Opening prayer
- Announcements
- A time to sing praise and worship
- The Word goes forth
- Time for MOG (the move of God)

- Alter call and Prayer
- Closing prayer

All in 50 minutes before the next herd of saints come in.

<u>AUTHOR NOTE:</u> *Because God Looks Upon The Heart, He Can Save and Use   Anybody at Anytime! I Respect all Styles of Ministry, as long as Christ is Lord!*

The Churches of Gyration and the Overly Emotional

These ministries mostly teach salvation only, and very little else. The preacher uses special breathing techniques (whooping) with the banging of the organ or the piano in the background. Don't be surprised if this preacher decides to bust a move or two, to really get the excitement going inside. Again, again and again the pulpit hits the people with a loud vocal and musical crescendo, till every soul is jumping, shaking and running up and down the aisles.

The Churches of Statutes

These churches are usually old and well established in the communities. Slowly and quietly the Saints file in with little smiles and welcoming nod or two. They take their seats with their feet and knees together, bibles in their laps, and their hands folded together on top. After being seated nobody looks around, eyes forward as the organ softly plays in the background, when the music stops the bishop, priest or the elder makes his way to a lofty alter and calls out a page number and reads a prayer out of a little black book, that's not a bible.

At the end of the reading, there was a low rumble that echoed and filled the room with the men's voices only, AAAA- men! Then sister so and so, in a big full white pleated dress, get up and sang in soprano, a beautiful, old, slow song. The same song it seems like she sang every Sunday for at least 30 years. The congregation sat in their long wooden pews and in unison, they kneeled down and stood up, they kneeled down and stood up again in unison and then sat down very quietly. From the lofty place someone spoke for a short time, in an amplified soft voice about Jesus and then stepped down. Then the low rumbling AAAA-men, came from the voices and then it's over.

The Church of Positive Thinking, Talking and Prosperity

Some saints need to feel like they have done a good thing by attending church. So they find a place where the music is dramatic, and upbeat and patriotic, then comes a feel good message. These preachers wax elegant, with melodious tones in their voices as they smile throughout their oratory. They may use a number of biblical verses that say, we must walk and talk in faith. Ask what so ever you will and it will be done unto you. This is similar to the churches of the over emotional, except these emotions are intellectual. It's like grit your teeth and keep repeating within yourself I think I can, I think I can, I think I can. Just like that little choo-choo train, in the children's story. What a man can conceive, a man can achieve. Sounds good so far, but the devil is in the left out details. What about the teaching of sin, repentance, sorrow and shame. The tragedies we bring upon ourselves, and rebellion, if you force yourself back into reality you can't chant, intellectualize, or self talk your way out of these universal failings of man.

When these immature, falsely taught Christians, get alone by themselves they feel the emotional highs in being in the mist of the masses, being drained away by the world during the week. These churches are teaching that when you are feeling low and on the edges of depression, read their books and listen to their tapes and DVD's. Use these, maybe not said (but implied) instead of going into fasting, or deep prayer or studying the bible by itself.

The Word of God teaches that all of us have sinned and come short. Our thoughts, our hearts and our flesh are wicked, proud and greedy (Proverbs 6:14 & 15:26-28). If we find the ability to control our own hearts and mind fully, then we would not need the Saving Mercy and Grace of God. Only after total submission and confession of sins and repentance, with the Lord Jesus being our personal Savior.

Only through him and the knowledge of his word will allow the promises, the purposes and the blessings to flow.

Author's Note:
The above four types of styles of churches are my own personal testimonies and observations over 50 years of my life. I was looking for the real God that spoke to my heart as a child. The God that saved my life, from certain death too numerous to count. From my imperfect parents, I saw firsthand their nomadic search for Him.

Around seven years old, from my dad I learned through example, for he was a man of few words. I saw the power of prayer and the peace of mind that he would have in his face, as his face shined every night, aAs he rose from his knees. All six of his kids watched him from the hallway, our father for at least one hour it seemed, prayed very quietly as he was on the floor talking to somebody. And my mother stood guard to make sure we all were perfectly still before we would get our kisses and hugs goodnight until my father arose.

Through my mom, I learned that my dad had a personal relationship with the Lord of heaven as he knew Him. My mother was the reader, she would read to us daily when we were awoke and at night when we were asleep. Over the years, my mom read every story of the bible to us. 15 or 20 years passed for our little clan; we visited almost every church within 25 miles of home.

We experienced many, many souls saved by Jesus in all of these styles or types of ministries. I knew that the Lord can use anybody willing to serve Him. My parents knew and used the bible as their one and only guide to find the God of the Old and New Testament. Man's churches in these latter days have too much fluff and stuff and gaudiness, with no or very little verse by verse teaching. The cults have too many secrets or too many rules and regulations that weren't biblically based.

So our family was home schooled or home churched if you will, in the Word of God, by God himself. By the way, my parents did find a bible based church to make their Spiritual Home for Fellowship.

I left on my own after that, to find my spiritual purpose, and I found it in the Bible. What I found is that the Lord wants an individual and personal relationship with all His True children. There is a style of ministry just for you. Faith comes by hearing, by hearing the Word Of God. Confess to The Lord JESUS and His Blood will cover your Sins and make you Sinless. His Mercy and His Grace will make you sin less. Find Your Style. Mine just happens to be a Home Church.

How Does The Love Grow Cold?

Did you know that there are different kinds of love? First, God is love (1 John 4:7-8), that's where we have to start. God has His own kind of love. In the Greek it's translated to the word ***Agape***, it's unconditional love or the hottest love, it is the love of all goodness and His glory. God's agape love doesn't need reciprocation. In the English language we're limited to one word, love. But in the Greek language there are four different words, one of which is the above agape.

Phileo - is a godly kind of love for man or a familiar love, even brotherly love. One of our major cities has the name Philadelphia, the city of brotherly love. *The last two are the lower humanistic types of love.*

Storge - is the love for things and the power it brings, like I love my car, or I love my home etc. The of love things have ran up our credit cards and has made us lose our homes and maybe even our families, and has put us in all kinds of debt. It's our worldly desires for stuff and things. We have a hard time separating and, or prioritizing our needs from our wants. This is an unprecedented time in history for all of mankind. The world's economy's, are so interlinked and woven together that evil forces using *storge* will cause nation after nation to pull one another down like a string of dominos.

Eros - is the erotic love, which appeals to our most base of nature. It is widely used around the world. It helps with the selling of everything from hamburgers to automobiles to every kind of luxury items you can imagine. The most eternal damning use of Erotic love, is the flesh and the smut peddlers of the world.

What the Lord meant for good, was only be shared by a husband and wife for procreation, enjoyment, and for the filling of the earth. Is now one of the Devil's main tools to cause the loss of productivity, addictions, rape, prostitutions, murders and the killings of unborn babies as a form of birth control.

In these last days the book of Isaiah 5:20 said it best, "Woe to those who call evil good and good for evil, who called darkness for light and light for darkness. Things that are bitter is sweet and the sweet is bitter."

Eros is being touted as the number one love. In our weaknesses it causes that first, fleshly lustful look, the first touch that burns with desires or that first out of control imagination that plays that mental video, with perfect sights and sounds, to fit the occasion. For men this is devastatingly real. For women it's put to erotic print, and the TV soaps and movies that pull within her, all of the right strings.

The Apostle Paul was very aware of demonic influences that are in the world. Paul wrote a letter to the Christian Churches in Galatia (modern Turkey), to Encourage and Rebuke them. Even warning them that their sins must stop right now, or they will be doomed to hell. He laid it out one by one so that there will be no excuses.

"Now the works of the flesh are manifest, which are these; Adultery, fornication, uncleanness, lasciviousness, idolatry, witchcraft, hatred, variance, emulations, wrath, strife, seditions, heresies, envyings, murders, drunkenness, revellings, and such like: of the which I tell you before, as I

have also told you in time past, that they which do such things shall not inherit the kingdom of God". Galatians 5:19-21

In these verses you'll find an itemized list of the Soul Damming Sins. Within these they are a promise to those who rebel against the Words of God. Because of the relentless years of poking and prodding, double entendres, and innuendoes. The American Christianity has been knocked down on its knees; the Devil has been able to fire every weapon in his arsenal to weaken the faithful. Every modern technology is in the hands of the **god of this world.**

Using *Storge* and *Eros* 1 John 2:15-16 mixed with the prides of men's hearts has now driven the Saints into a cold love for God, because of their hopelessness. Also, many churches conformed to a worldly model of lukewarmness an all inclusiveness from every religion. Welcoming everybody and their Sins, have made them become the churches of social networking.

In this book we have a ministry to teach those who have not given in, nor given up in the Lord. You can still read, study and grow in the Lord, right from home. As you and your family get stronger and stronger, we'll help you find a community driven church, still on its knees praying for Mature Saints, ready to come in for the battle ahead, to save the lost.

"And when they were departed, behold, the angel of the Lord appeareth to Joseph in a dream, saying Arise and take the young child and his mother, and flee to Egypt; and be thou there until I bring thee word: for Herod will seek the young child to destroy him. v14 When he arose, he took the young child and his mother by night, and departed into Egypt". (Matthew 2: 13-14)

God is looking for men and women especially families, to become his living sacrifices, to be holy and pleasing to Him.

"I beseech you therefore, brethren, by the mercies of God, that ye present your bodies a living sacrifice, holy, acceptable unto God, which is your

reasonable service. v2. And be not conformed to this world: but be ye transformed by the renewing of your mind, that ye may prove what is that good, and acceptable, and perfect will of God". (Romans 12:1-2)

Starting at your home, we learn to worship, no longer conforming to this world. We allow the Spirit of God and His Word to renew our minds, so much so, we will be able to pass any test thrown at us, because that is His Will for us. When we please the Lord our Creator, that is our reasonable service back to Him.

CHAPTER SEVEN

Building a House That Will Please the Lord

Yes, this is a loaded question. In Acts 7:49-50 it states; *"Heaven is my throne, and earth is my footstool: what house will you build me? says the Lord: or what is the place of my rest?"*

Unless the Lord builds the house, its builders labor in vain. Unless the Lord watches over the city, the watchmen stand guard in vain. Psalms 127:1 NIV

    Man has always thought that if he built great Cathedrals and Temples, it would help him get closer to God. He believed, by using the world's best talents and materials, he would somehow make his building be a Holy place of worship. Yes, just like the tower of Babel, man's pride set into the hearts of its people, and the spirits of darkness turned man's futile thoughts into thinking that tower, would reach God's Heaven, if they could only build it tall enough.

    For now, let's talk about what The Church is not. Because of the weaknesses of man's flesh and pride, it opened the door for the Devil to rush in with all kinds of sins. When the Holy Spirit leaves a ministry, all you're left with is nothing but a social club or an organization. Nowadays, you have to attend the right church.

    Some of our Presidents of the United States used Sunday, mornings as a photo opportunity, to be seen going to certain churches, carrying big Bibles. But before the elections our current President said that he was as Christian and that he would go to church. But now we find that his latest statement is; *"that going to church in Washington DC would be too disruptive for the fellow believers and surrounding communities"*. I am not casting judgment either way on this, but I do know that there are too many people who try to keep up appearances, in going to church just for the show of it. They do it because they think it is the right thing to do. Some attend because they made a promise to someone or they were forced or threatened with mental or physical pain by a dominating love one.

There are churches to fit every weakness of the flesh. Here is a list: We have homosexual congregations, a church of swingers, we have racist churches of hate. Passive congregations that just huddle in their masses, they don't want to do anything but just wait for the end to come. The cults have secrets of all kinds, churches with chants and vain babblings. Idol worships, smoke, fire and the burning incense and herbs. They have the mystics and séances, the palm readers, the tarot card readers.

Some vocalize the science of the mind. Those who worship the dead and their bones, like voodoo worship, the sacrificing of animals and the worshipping of Satan himself.

So to counteract these offenses of men, men devise and imagine without truly consulting the living God in prayer and study. They devise even more and more religions and denominations. For the last 70 to 80 years now, there has been an explosion of manmade religions and cults all over the world. America has most of them it seems, no wonder people are confused and don't know where to go, and that's real.

In our modern society, the new word for success is networking. And the so called church houses are filled with people, who are the buyers and the sellers, the movers and the shakers are all there at one time. But I recall only two places in the Bible where God had man to construct a place of worship, one was portable, for the Israelites to travel from Egypt to the Promise Land. The other was built by King Solomon who spent million and million in its construction.

It is my opinion, that when Jesus hung on that tree and when the spear pierced His side, His blood was shed for the remission of sins and you'll find that in Hebrews 9:22. When Jesus' blood hit the ground, the whole world became a suitable place for God to be worshipped.

Today with much Pomp and Circumstance, men and their religions, strut like proud peacocks, say without saying; "look at me and honor me and the position I hold". What happened to our Godly Humility? Jesus washed the disciples feet, and you'll find in Mark 10:44-45. He said; *"whoever wants to be first, must be a servant to all. He himself did not come to this earth to be served but to serve, and gave His life for a ransom for many".*

I submit to you, that if Jesus Christ is your Lord and Savior YOU ARE GOD'S TEMPLE. "If you're in a plane, you can call on His name, if you're on the ocean, His feelings for you are more than a notion, if you're on the earth, He can give you rebirth." We can pray and worship God at any time at any place.

"Don't you know that you yourselves are God's temple and that God's Spirit lives in you?" 1 Corinthians 3:16. *"The god who made the world and everything in it is the Lord of Heaven and earth, and does not live in temples built by hands".* Acts 17:24

In the Last Days, the Lord is bringing back an old idea, the HOME CHURCH. *Remember ye not the former things, neither consider the things of old. Behold, I will do a new thing; now it shall spring forth; shall ye not know it? I will even make a way in the wilderness, and rivers in the desert.* (Isaiah 43: 18-19)

Just by the virtue of being a Home Church, automatically brings people closer together and strengthens relationships. It will bring a stronger sense of community, not to mention what it will do for the families that live in your area. Maybe the word will get out that your house and your family stands for something.

Your light will be Shining and your Salt will be a Preserving Flavor in the eyes of those who watch.

HOME CHURCHES INTERNATIONAL was design by God Himself to reach out to the unchurched and those who have been discouraged, disillusioned, disgraced, discredited or discriminated by the traditional churches, real or imaged. Sometimes these people hold their religion higher than the relationships of their members.

Please understand, I know, that there is thousands of fine, Loving Bible teaching traditional churches, all across the country and around the world. I do not want to cast shadows of doubt on them all. As a matter of fact, before I wrote this book and started this ministry, I was a regular member of a very loving church in Riverside, California that had about 4,000 members. But you have to agree, that for every church on fire for God there is one lukewarm or stone cold. Who by their complacency has become comfortable in their Christianity, thus puts the world in its condition today.

Today's world, needs strong saints who will stand up and take the challenge, administering a heavy dose of God's love. We need to be more intimate than ever. We need to be able and have the freedom to cry, on one another's shoulder. Men in Christ need to be taught what it means to be a man, and to lead his family Spiritually.

When we learn to "love the Lord our God with all our heart, with all our soul and with all our mind, we would have completed the first of the greatest commandments. In order to complete God's second commandment, thereby fulfilling your destiny and calling in Christ, you are to "LOVE YOUR NEIGHBORS, AS YOU LOVE YOURSELVES". (Matthew 22:36-40)

I hope that the main points we studied in the book of Acts, helped you to understand the backbone of this ministry. It's a calling from the heart of God. It's perfectly adaptable and strategic for these perilous times. As these times get worse and worse the Home Churches will be the last line of defense before the Great Persecution comes.

We believe that by having a church in our home, keeps pride down to a minimum. Everyone in Christ has something to offer. Your ministry is a gift from God, that if shared can encourage and uplift someone in the faith, and by doing so makes you a leader.

We do not try, nor do we want to compete against larger churches. The first churches started in the book of Acts, they did not seem to have bands and choirs, but what they did have, was the Power of the Holy Spirit to do miracles.

Maybe it takes more faith to stay in a small ministry, where you will be forced to grow in Christ Jesus.

By no means will we discourage anyone from leaving this ministry. We really hope that after one grows into a certain point of maturity in the Lord, that he would start a HOME CHURCH in his or her own home. Not only would you receive our blessings and guidance, you will also receive our help with the administration.

If one wants to simply move into another ministry, feel free with our blessings, just stay in the Word of God and in the Body of Christ.

For the most of us this is a true fact. We spend more time in our homes, living our lives than any other place. So In our dwelling places among family and friends where we are truly ourselves, let us get closer to the LORD. Quite naturally from the Lord's perspective, we'll be judged the most from there, first anyway. So let's get it right and keep it real, with our Savior.

We should pray. Jesus, help us restart our faith and build a deeper relationship with you, in our home. This will please Him.

CHAPTER EIGHT

How Do We Get Started?

Today's traditional or modern churches, consists of large buildings where many scores, and hundreds and even thousands of worshippers come together. It is sad to say that a vast majority of these believers are there to hide among the numbers, never intending to pray, study or spread the Gospel. They are there to make themselves better, just for a moment, never letting what was said or what was read to take root in their hearts. There are untold millions of people who believe in God, but because of sin, the lack of priorities and the cares of this world are virtually indistinguishable from the worldly non-believers.

Out of guilt, shame and the weight of sin, these same people are forced by their consciences to pack into our churches and synagogues on Easter (Passover) and Christmas. These pew warmers and sporadic attendees fill the seats of our traditional churches with empty hearts. These are the ones I believe Home Churches International will reach because of your love and prayers. They are your neighbors to your left or to your right and across the street they are your mothers, fathers, sisters and brothers. With your divine calling and the Lord's anointing upon your life, He has strategically placed you, right in the middle of these souls that only you can reach. When you open up your Home Church to break bread and share your love with them and the Gospel of our Lord and Savior Jesus Christ they will come, and will be saved.

It always starts with prayer, this will be a new permanent commitment until death do we part or Jesus' second coming. It is His perfect will for families to read, study, pray, give, worship, fellowship and serve the Lord 24/7/365 from our homes and everywhere else. This is where we all must start, it's a no brainer. What you may not know right away is, the Lord's deeper calling on your life. You could be a full service, fully anointed Church by God, an independent ministry, but totally dependent upon the Holy Spirit. I know all of this can be a little shocking to your soul at first, but let's not get to far ahead of ourselves, our job is to help you K.I.S.S. it. **K**eep **I**t **S**imple **S**illy, we'll provide for you a spiritual covering for accountability, study notes and even a correspondence course to guide you through Biblical doctrine. The Holy Spirit will lead you through the rest.

However, fast or slow you want to go, we'll be right there for you. If you already know you are called to be a Pastor, we have the time and the expertise to help you as well.

Start with as little as 15 minutes, then choose one specific day of the week and one designated room in your house then be consistent. Once you have started, it will seem like everything will breakout against you, to stop you from this new commitment to God.

Remember, God calls the one in the family that has the deepest and most sincere relationship with Him. So after you have started this time of devotion, don't get discouraged if it's only you for awhile in attendance. Believe me, you are being watched to see if you are serious and faithful. The Lord's Holy Spirit will bring conviction and repentance to their hearts.

As the Lord's servant, you'll become that spiritual rock in the family and the Spirit of God will draw them to you to show them what to do next. Don't worry, be strong and very courageous, we don't wrestle against flesh and blood (Ephesians 6:12). Remember this and study this, and you will be **victorious**.

"Be strong and of good courage: for unto this people shalt thou divide for an inheritance the land, which I sware unto their fathers to give them. v7. Only be thou strong and very courageous, that thou mayest observe to do according to all the law, which Moses my servant commanded thee: turn not from it to the right hand or to the left, that thou mayest prosper whithersoever thou goest. v8. This book of the law shall not depart out of thy mouth; but thou shall meditate therein day and night, that thou mayest observe to do according to all that is written therein: for then

thou shalt make thy way prosperous, and then thou shalt have good success. v9. Have not I commanded thee? Be strong and of good courage; be not afraid, neither be thou dismayed: for the Lord thy God is with thee whithersoever thou goest.
(Joshua 1:6-9)

For a season, however long it is there are at least five Wills/Wheels of God, commanded to be at work in all of His churches. Let's take a car, unless all five wheels are being utilized, (you have four on the ground and one steering wheel), it is good for nothing but it's still a car, right. Christians are commanded by His word to:

1. Pray
2. Study
3. Fellowship
4. To give
5. To serve the Lord

A true believer must be a doer, all these (Wills/Wheels) to be used in His Perfect Will. If not, you're still saved, but just being used maybe sometimes, in His permissive will. This could be a lukewarm condition and even dangerous, for your eternal soul. So once again, as you are continuing with your home ministry and still maturing on an individual basis, that's good. And by now, you should have grown into your spiritual gift of discernment. If you find it hard to completely fulfill the five Wills/Wheels commandments and some of the other spiritual gifts 1 Corinthians 12:1 & 8-12 are not present along with the ministry gifts in Ephesians 4:11-12 maybe it's time for you to find a Corporate Church Body to be a part of and we can help you with that as well.

For you Home Church pastors that are ready to go (please join our free family membership) please pray and fast about this lifelong commitment. The Lord holds we pastors to a higher standard.

"My brethren, be not many masters, knowing that we shall receive the greater condemnation". (James 3:1)

So we must be living examples of Christ in every way possible. In Ephesians 4:11-12 we must have one or more of these ministry gifts.

In 1 Corinthians 12: 1& 8-12, you must have two or more of these spiritual gifts. The two, being at least Faith, and the gift to Discern spirits. We must know Jesus Christ and His Word personally and intimately, like He knows and loves us unconditionally.

"Study to shew thyself approved unto God, a workman that needeth not to be ashamed, rightly dividing the word of truth". (2 Timothy 2: 15)

We're called to be the overseers of the souls of men here on earth, from the womb to the tomb. This is a great and awesome responsibility. Therefore, the Lord promised, that He would not put something on us beyond our ability to handle. You will gain more wisdom, strength and power as you exercise more righteousness and humility towards your congregation.

"Obey them that have the rule over you, and submit yourselves: for they watch for your souls, as they that must give account, that they may do it with joy, and not with grief: for that is unprofitable for you". (Hebrews 13:17)

PRAYER FOR SALVATION AND PEACE

**** Please Pray First Then Study Scriptures ****

Romans 3:3-4 Let all men be a lie but God and his Word, is the Truth

Romans 3:23 All have sinned, and come short of God's Glory.

Romans 6:23 The wages of sin is death, the gift of God, is eternal life.

Romans 5:19 One man's disobedience (Adam) brought sin, one other men (Jesus / God) brought Righteousness unto Salvation.

Romans 10:9-10 Confess with your mouth and believe in your heart the LORD JESUS unto Salvation.

Romans 6:22 Being free from sin, you'll produce good fruit, and have Everlasting life as a Servant of God.

2 Cor. 5:17 Those in Christ, become new people, old things are passed away, all things become new.

Phil 4:7 God's Peace is beyond your understanding, it will keep your Heart and mind through Christ Jesus.

We hope this book has helped you catch the vision before our Lord and Savior returns to the earth.

HOME CHURCHES INTERNATIONAL: is for anyone, man or woman that has the burning desire to get God's Word out, into their homes and neighborhood. We will show you how, step by step. For more information, on our Study Guides, Discipleship Programs and Correspondence Course.

ABOUT THE AUTHOR

THE PURPOSE AND MEANING OF LIFE

At age 40, I found myself looking inside my heart and taking as account of earthly possessions and personal accomplishments. Quite frankly I wasn't where I wanted to be or doing what I knew I was capable of doing. I knew that God gave me gifts and talents. The rude awakening was that I was trying to do all these great things without truly serving the one that gave the talents in the first place. In September 1982, I founded my 1st Church in Los Angeles County. For almost two years things went well but in my zeal to serve the Lord and being a young Christian, I found out that I have bitten off more than I could chew. It was a 24/7/365 day job. That is when I swore to myself that I would never be a Pastor again. It wasn't until I married my wife Vivian in 1995 that the Lord rekindled my love for Him. He gave me a burden for the Souls of men. Teaching them how to escape Hell, that was only created for the fallen Angels.

In a way that only the Lord can, He spoke to my heart, saying, "The Call for you to be My Servant was not a mistake". I just missed His timing.

One more year passed after that. Using much prayer and fasting, together with my wife, I knew it was time to step out into the deep. We started October 25th, 1996 the ministry of Home Churches International. In our home with six people HCI was born.

I am a Teacher not a Preacher (for the most part). I break the Bible which is the Word of God, down into everyday language so the young and old can understand. God has principles for our health, wealth and overall prosperity.

"What profits a man to gain the whole world and to lose his own soul," Mark 8:36. What that means is God is an Eternal Being and believe it or not, we are created in His image and we are eternal beings as well. For HIS pleasure, Adam and Eve were meant to walk and talk with GOD forever. The LORD GOD and HIS Children Living in a perfect place with perfect weather for an eternity. Well as we all know, they messed that up!

So now we're in his testing ground called, LIFE, however long it is, from 0-100, IT IS JUST THE BEGINNING OF OUR ETERNAL LIFE. Life is choices. What you choose or don't choose, things good or things bad is going to be held against you. Life was meant to be hard without JESUS. Why do you think it's called **"SALVATION"**. Saved from yourself, flesh, the Devil and Hell. I know you have questions. I would LOVE to help you make The right eternal CHOICE!

It's still hard work and 24/7/365 days a year. But now I know my PURPOSE and the MEANING OF LIFE. The **Purpose is to Seek HIM** in the Bible and He'll show you His perfect timing for everything that concerns you. The **Meaning of Life is to please the LORD.** Make HIM Look Good, by the way I walk, talk, and live life in Private as well as in Public. *What is your PURPOSE AND MEANING?* Are you still trying to do great things in this life, **WITHOUT** *truly serving* **The ONE** that gave those gifts and talents?

Please Call or Write

E-mail: hci1million@gmail.com

Check Here For Broadcast Times and Schedule
Website: www.homechurchesinternational.org

Blog: www.homechurchesonline.org

Mailing Address: P.O. BOX 3388, Riverside, CA 92519
Phone Number: 951-360-3399